LTL

6/03

Australia

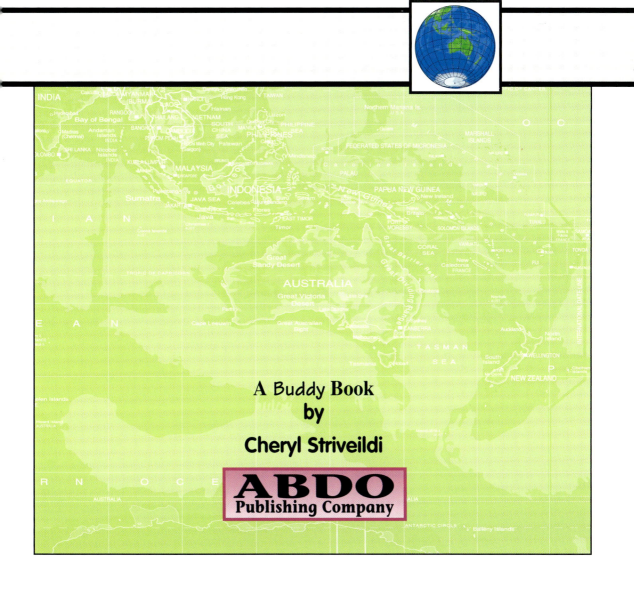

A Buddy Book
by

Cheryl Striveildi

ABDO
Publishing Company

VISIT US AT
www.abdopub.com

Published by Buddy Books, an imprint of ABDO Publishing Company, 4940 Viking Drive, Edina, Minnesota 55435. Copyright © 2003 by Abdo Consulting Group, Inc. International copyrights reserved in all countries. No part of this book may be reproduced in any form without written permission from the publisher.

Printed in the United States.

Edited by: Christy DeVillier
Contributing Editors: Matt Ray, Michael P. Goecke
Graphic Design: M. Hosley
Image Research: Deborah Coldiron
Photographs: Corbis, Corel, Digital Stock, Minden Pictures, PhotoEssentials, Dr. Acram Taji (University of New England, Armidale, New South Wales, Australia)

Library of Congress Cataloging-in-Publication Data

Striveildi, Cheryl, 1971-
   Continents. Australia / Cheryl Striveildi.
      p. cm.
   Includes index.
   Summary: A very brief introduction to the geography, climate, plants, and animals of Australia.
   ISBN 1-57765-961-9
      1. Australia—Juvenile literature. [1. Australia.] I. Title: Australia. II. Title.

DU96 .S74 2003
919.4—dc21

                               2002074661

Table of Contents

Seven Continents

Water covers most of the earth. Land covers the rest. The earth has seven main land areas, or **continents**. The seven continents are:

 North America

 Africa

 South America

 Asia

 Europe

 Australia

 Antarctica

Australia is an exciting place.

Australia is the smallest **continent**. It covers about 2,978,100 square miles (7,713,243 sq km). It is about the size of the United States.

Australia is like nowhere else in the world. Kangaroos, koalas, and other interesting animals live there. Australia also has fine beaches and cities. This warm continent is an exciting place to be.

Where Is Australia?

A **hemisphere** is half of the earth. The top half of the earth is the Northern Hemisphere. The Southern Hemisphere is the bottom half of the earth. Australia is in the Southern Hemisphere. This is why some people call Australia the Land Down Under.

The main part of Australia is an island. It has water on all sides. Australia lies between the Indian Ocean and the Pacific Ocean.

Tasmania is also part of Australia. It is a smaller island to the south.

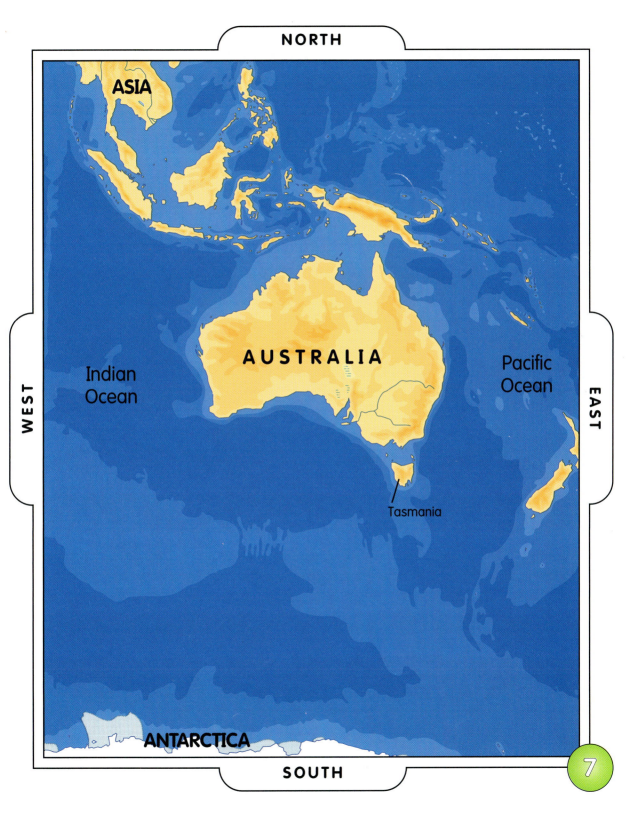

ASIA

AUSTRALIA

Indian
Ocean

Pacific
Ocean

Tasmania

ANTARCTICA

Sixth-Largest Country

There is only one country on the **continent** of Australia. It is also called Australia. It is the sixth-largest country in the world. Australia's six states and two territories are:

- New South Wales
- Victoria
- Queensland
- South Australia
- Western Australia
- Tasmania
- Northern Territory
- Australian Capital Territory

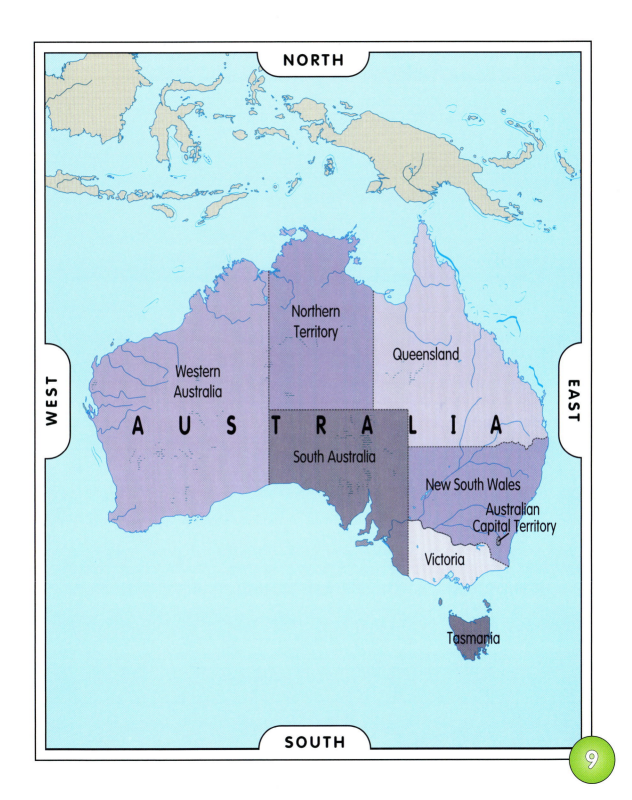

NORTH

WEST

EAST

SOUTH

Northern
Territory

Queensland

Western
Australia

A U S T R A L I A

South Australia

New South Wales

Australian
Capital Territory

Victoria

Tasmania

9

Sydney is a city on
Australia's east coast.

Australia's full name is the Commonwealth of Australia. The common language of Australia is English. About 18 million people live in Australia. Most Australians live near the coast.

Aborigines

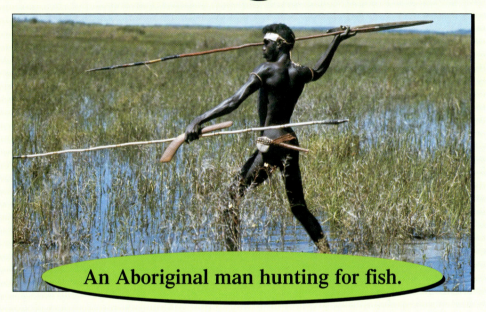

An Aboriginal man hunting for fish.

The first Australians were Aborigines. They came to Australia about 40,000 years ago. The Aborigines hunted animals and gathered plants for food. Many of them died when Europeans came to Australia. More than 300,000 Aboriginal people live in Australia today.

Western Plateau

Australia's Western **Plateau** begins in the west and covers most of Australia. The center of the Western Plateau is very dry. It is the driest part of Australia. Few people live there. This dry land is called Australia's outback.

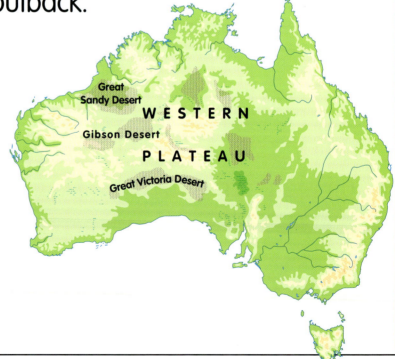

Great Sandy Desert

WESTERN

Gibson Desert

PLATEAU

Great Victoria Desert

Much of the Western Plateau is very dry.

Deserts get less than 10 inches (25 cm) of rain each year. Australia's Western **Plateau** has three main deserts:

- Great Sandy Desert
- Gibson Desert
- Great Victoria Desert

Australia's desert land is not good for farming. But wild plants can grow there. Two desert flowers are the kangaroo paw and the sturt desert pea. They bloom after desert rains.

Sturt desert pea

Desert tree

Kangaroo paw

Central Lowlands

East of the Western **Plateau** are the Central Lowlands. The Central Lowlands and the Western Plateau are mostly flat. In fact, Australia is the flattest **continent**.

The lowest land of Australia is in the Central Lowlands. Australia's lowest point is Lake Eyre. Lake Eyre is not always full of water. Many of Australia's lakes stay dry for years.

A cattle ranch in Australia

The Central Lowlands have flat, grassy land. This grassy land is good for raising sheep and cattle. But this land is too dry for farming.

East Coast

Many cities are on Australia's east coast. A few of them are Brisbane, Sydney, and Canberra. Canberra is Australia's capital city. Sydney has more people than any other city in Australia.

Brisbane

Sydney

Canberra

Brisbane, Australia

The Eastern Highlands lie along Australia's east coast. This land area has **plateaus**, hills, and mountains. The Blue Mountains and the Australian Alps are there. Mount Kosciusko is in the Australian Alps. Its **peak** is the highest point in Australia.

Australian Alps

Australia's Seasons

Australia's seasons are like North America's seasons. But they happen at different times of the year. Australians enjoy summer when North Americans have winter. Australia's summer happens in December, January, and February. Australia's winter happens in June, July, and August.

Winter in Victoria, Australia

The Eucalyptus

Australia is famous for its hardwood eucalyptus trees. Eucalyptus trees are sometimes called gum trees. People use these hardwood trees to build houses and furniture. Eucalyptus oil is important, too. It is used in medicine, soap, and cleaning supplies.

Eucalyptus forest

Animals

Australia has animals unlike any others in the world. One is the duck-billed platypus. This animal has a beak like a duck's. But it is not a bird. The duck-billed platypus also has webbed feet. It lives in and near water.

Duck-billed platypus

Australia is famous for **marsupial** animals. Female marsupials carry their babies in a special pouch. Koalas, wombats, and kangaroos are marsupials.

Wombat

Koalas

A mother kangaroo and her baby

Emu

Kookaburra

Australia has many kinds of uncommon birds. There are kookaburras, colorful parrots, and emus. Emus are the second-largest birds in the world. They can grow to become six feet (two m) tall. Emus cannot fly. But they can run as fast as 30 mph (48 kph).

Spiny Anteater

Another strange Australian animal is the echidna. It has spines on most of its body. Another name for the echidna is spiny anteater. They eat ants and termites.

Visiting Australia

Thousands of people visit Australia's Great Barrier Reef each year. It is the world's largest **coral** reef. It is off Australia's northeast coast. This reef has more than 1,200 miles (1,931 km) of coral.

The Great Barrier Reef is made of living and dead coral. Coral are sea animals. The reef's living coral is colorful and very beautiful.

Many sea animals live near the Great Barrier Reef.

Australia's Great Barrier Reef
is made of coral.

Ayer's Rock

Another beautiful part of Australia is
Uluru. Uluru, or Ayer's Rock, is in the
outback. This rock is about 1,141 feet (348 m)
tall. Sunshine makes Ayer's Rock look
red. Its color changes throughout the day.

Australia's cities are full of interesting sights, too. People often visit the famous Sydney Opera House.

Sydney Opera House

Australia

- Australia is the smallest **continent**.

- Australia is the driest continent after Antarctica.

- About 18 million people live in Australia.

- Most Australians speak English.

- The Murray-Darling is the longest river in Australia.

- The highest point in Australia is Mount Kosciusko.

- Australia's lowest point is Lake Eyre.

- The native people of Australia are called Aborigines.

Important Words

continent one of the earth's seven main land areas.

coral tiny sea animals and their hard bones.

hemisphere one half of the earth.

marsupial a kind of animal. Female marsupials have a special pouch for carrying newborn young.

peak mountaintop.

plateau flat land that is higher than the land around it.

Web Sites

Would you like to learn more about Australia?
Please visit ABDO Publishing Company on the World Wide Web to find web site links about Australia. These links are routinely monitored and updated to provide the most current information available.

www.abdopub.com

Index